I0474714

THIS SHIT BELONGS TO

A

WEBSITE

USERNAME

PASSWORD

NOTES

WEBSITE

USERNAME

PASSWORD

NOTES

WEBSITE

USERNAME

PASSWORD

NOTES

WEBSITE

USERNAME

PASSWORD

NOTES

WEBSITE

USERNAME

PASSWORD

NOTES

WEBSITE

USERNAME

PASSWORD

NOTES

A

WEBSITE

USERNAME

PASSWORD

NOTES

WEBSITE

USERNAME

PASSWORD

NOTES

WEBSITE

USERNAME

PASSWORD

NOTES

WEBSITE

USERNAME

PASSWORD

NOTES

WEBSITE

USERNAME

PASSWORD

NOTES

WEBSITE

USERNAME

PASSWORD

NOTES

B

WEBSITE

USERNAME

PASSWORD

NOTES

WEBSITE

USERNAME

PASSWORD

NOTES

WEBSITE

USERNAME

PASSWORD

NOTES

WEBSITE

USERNAME

PASSWORD

NOTES

WEBSITE

USERNAME

PASSWORD

NOTES

WEBSITE

USERNAME

PASSWORD

NOTES

B

WEBSITE

USERNAME

PASSWORD

NOTES

WEBSITE

USERNAME

PASSWORD

NOTES

WEBSITE

USERNAME

PASSWORD

NOTES

B

WEBSITE

USERNAME

PASSWORD

NOTES

WEBSITE

USERNAME

PASSWORD

NOTES

WEBSITE

USERNAME

PASSWORD

NOTES

C

WEBSITE

USERNAME

PASSWORD

NOTES

WEBSITE

USERNAME

PASSWORD

NOTES

WEBSITE

USERNAME

PASSWORD

NOTES

WEBSITE

USERNAME

PASSWORD

NOTES

WEBSITE

USERNAME

PASSWORD

NOTES

WEBSITE

USERNAME

PASSWORD

NOTES

C

WEBSITE

USERNAME

PASSWORD

NOTES

WEBSITE

USERNAME

PASSWORD

NOTES

WEBSITE

USERNAME

PASSWORD

NOTES

WEBSITE

USERNAME

PASSWORD

NOTES

WEBSITE

USERNAME

PASSWORD

NOTES

WEBSITE

USERNAME

PASSWORD

NOTES

D

WEBSITE

USERNAME

PASSWORD

NOTES

WEBSITE

USERNAME

PASSWORD

NOTES

WEBSITE

USERNAME

PASSWORD

NOTES

WEBSITE

USERNAME

PASSWORD

NOTES

WEBSITE

USERNAME

PASSWORD

NOTES

WEBSITE

USERNAME

PASSWORD

NOTES

D

WEBSITE

USERNAME

PASSWORD

NOTES

WEBSITE

USERNAME

PASSWORD

NOTES

WEBSITE

USERNAME

PASSWORD

NOTES

WEBSITE

USERNAME

PASSWORD

NOTES

WEBSITE

USERNAME

PASSWORD

NOTES

WEBSITE

USERNAME

PASSWORD

NOTES

WEBSITE

USERNAME

PASSWORD

NOTES

WEBSITE

USERNAME

PASSWORD

NOTES

WEBSITE

USERNAME

PASSWORD

NOTES

WEBSITE

USERNAME

PASSWORD

NOTES

WEBSITE

USERNAME

PASSWORD

NOTES

WEBSITE

USERNAME

PASSWORD

NOTES

**E**

WEBSITE

USERNAME

PASSWORD

NOTES

WEBSITE

USERNAME

PASSWORD

NOTES

WEBSITE

USERNAME

PASSWORD

NOTES

WEBSITE

USERNAME

PASSWORD

NOTES

WEBSITE

USERNAME

PASSWORD

NOTES

WEBSITE

USERNAME

PASSWORD

NOTES

F

WEBSITE

USERNAME

PASSWORD

NOTES

WEBSITE

USERNAME

PASSWORD

NOTES

WEBSITE

USERNAME

PASSWORD

NOTES

WEBSITE

USERNAME

PASSWORD

NOTES

WEBSITE

USERNAME

PASSWORD

NOTES

WEBSITE

USERNAME

PASSWORD

NOTES

F

WEBSITE

USERNAME

PASSWORD

NOTES

WEBSITE

USERNAME

PASSWORD

NOTES

WEBSITE

USERNAME

PASSWORD

NOTES

WEBSITE

USERNAME

PASSWORD

NOTES

WEBSITE

USERNAME

PASSWORD

NOTES

WEBSITE

USERNAME

PASSWORD

NOTES

G

WEBSITE

USERNAME

PASSWORD

NOTES

WEBSITE

USERNAME

PASSWORD

NOTES

WEBSITE

USERNAME

PASSWORD

NOTES

WEBSITE

USERNAME

PASSWORD

NOTES

WEBSITE

USERNAME

PASSWORD

NOTES

WEBSITE

USERNAME

PASSWORD

NOTES

G

WEBSITE

USERNAME

PASSWORD

NOTES

WEBSITE

USERNAME

PASSWORD

NOTES

WEBSITE

USERNAME

PASSWORD

NOTES

WEBSITE

USERNAME

PASSWORD

NOTES

WEBSITE

USERNAME

PASSWORD

NOTES

WEBSITE

USERNAME

PASSWORD

NOTES

WEBSITE

USERNAME

PASSWORD

NOTES

WEBSITE

USERNAME

PASSWORD

NOTES

WEBSITE

USERNAME

PASSWORD

NOTES

WEBSITE

USERNAME

PASSWORD

NOTES

WEBSITE

USERNAME

PASSWORD

NOTES

WEBSITE

USERNAME

PASSWORD

NOTES

H

WEBSITE

USERNAME

PASSWORD

NOTES

WEBSITE

USERNAME

PASSWORD

NOTES

WEBSITE

USERNAME

PASSWORD

NOTES

WEBSITE

USERNAME

PASSWORD

NOTES

WEBSITE

USERNAME

PASSWORD

NOTES

WEBSITE

USERNAME

PASSWORD

NOTES

WEBSITE

USERNAME

PASSWORD

NOTES

WEBSITE

USERNAME

PASSWORD

NOTES

WEBSITE

USERNAME

PASSWORD

NOTES

WEBSITE

USERNAME

PASSWORD

NOTES

WEBSITE

USERNAME

PASSWORD

NOTES

WEBSITE

USERNAME

PASSWORD

NOTES

WEBSITE

USERNAME

PASSWORD

NOTES

WEBSITE

USERNAME

PASSWORD

NOTES

WEBSITE

USERNAME

PASSWORD

NOTES

WEBSITE

USERNAME

PASSWORD

NOTES

WEBSITE

USERNAME

PASSWORD

NOTES

WEBSITE

USERNAME

PASSWORD

NOTES

J

WEBSITE

USERNAME

PASSWORD

NOTES

WEBSITE

USERNAME

PASSWORD

NOTES

WEBSITE

USERNAME

PASSWORD

NOTES

WEBSITE

USERNAME

PASSWORD

NOTES

WEBSITE

USERNAME

PASSWORD

NOTES

WEBSITE

USERNAME

PASSWORD

NOTES

J

WEBSITE

USERNAME

PASSWORD

NOTES

WEBSITE

USERNAME

PASSWORD

NOTES

WEBSITE

USERNAME

PASSWORD

NOTES

WEBSITE

USERNAME

PASSWORD

NOTES

WEBSITE

USERNAME

PASSWORD

NOTES

WEBSITE

USERNAME

PASSWORD

NOTES

K

WEBSITE

USERNAME

PASSWORD

NOTES

WEBSITE

USERNAME

PASSWORD

NOTES

WEBSITE

USERNAME

PASSWORD

NOTES

WEBSITE

USERNAME

PASSWORD

NOTES

WEBSITE

USERNAME

PASSWORD

NOTES

WEBSITE

USERNAME

PASSWORD

NOTES

 K

WEBSITE

USERNAME

PASSWORD

NOTES

WEBSITE

USERNAME

PASSWORD

NOTES

WEBSITE

USERNAME

PASSWORD

NOTES

WEBSITE

USERNAME

PASSWORD

NOTES

WEBSITE

USERNAME

PASSWORD

NOTES

WEBSITE

USERNAME

PASSWORD

NOTES

L

WEBSITE

USERNAME

PASSWORD

NOTES

WEBSITE

USERNAME

PASSWORD

NOTES

WEBSITE

USERNAME

PASSWORD

NOTES

WEBSITE

USERNAME

PASSWORD

NOTES

WEBSITE

USERNAME

PASSWORD

NOTES

WEBSITE

USERNAME

PASSWORD

NOTES

L

WEBSITE

USERNAME

PASSWORD

NOTES

WEBSITE

USERNAME

PASSWORD

NOTES

WEBSITE

USERNAME

PASSWORD

NOTES

WEBSITE

USERNAME

PASSWORD

NOTES

WEBSITE

USERNAME

PASSWORD

NOTES

WEBSITE

USERNAME

PASSWORD

NOTES

M

WEBSITE

USERNAME

PASSWORD

NOTES

WEBSITE

USERNAME

PASSWORD

NOTES

WEBSITE

USERNAME

PASSWORD

NOTES

WEBSITE

USERNAME

PASSWORD

NOTES

WEBSITE

USERNAME

PASSWORD

NOTES

WEBSITE

USERNAME

PASSWORD

NOTES

M

WEBSITE

USERNAME

PASSWORD

NOTES

WEBSITE

USERNAME

PASSWORD

NOTES

WEBSITE

USERNAME

PASSWORD

NOTES

WEBSITE

USERNAME

PASSWORD

NOTES

WEBSITE

USERNAME

PASSWORD

NOTES

WEBSITE

USERNAME

PASSWORD

NOTES

N

WEBSITE

USERNAME

PASSWORD

NOTES

WEBSITE

USERNAME

PASSWORD

NOTES

WEBSITE

USERNAME

PASSWORD

NOTES

WEBSITE

USERNAME

PASSWORD

NOTES

WEBSITE

USERNAME

PASSWORD

NOTES

WEBSITE

USERNAME

PASSWORD

NOTES

N

WEBSITE

USERNAME

PASSWORD

NOTES

WEBSITE

USERNAME

PASSWORD

NOTES

WEBSITE

USERNAME

PASSWORD

NOTES

WEBSITE

USERNAME

PASSWORD

NOTES

WEBSITE

USERNAME

PASSWORD

NOTES

WEBSITE

USERNAME

PASSWORD

NOTES

WEBSITE

USERNAME

PASSWORD

NOTES

WEBSITE

USERNAME

PASSWORD

NOTES

WEBSITE

USERNAME

PASSWORD

NOTES

WEBSITE

USERNAME

PASSWORD

NOTES

WEBSITE

USERNAME

PASSWORD

NOTES

WEBSITE

USERNAME

PASSWORD

NOTES

WEBSITE

USERNAME

PASSWORD

NOTES

WEBSITE

USERNAME

PASSWORD

NOTES

WEBSITE

USERNAME

PASSWORD

NOTES

WEBSITE

USERNAME

PASSWORD

NOTES

WEBSITE

USERNAME

PASSWORD

NOTES

WEBSITE

USERNAME

PASSWORD

NOTES

P

WEBSITE

USERNAME

PASSWORD

NOTES

WEBSITE

USERNAME

PASSWORD

NOTES

WEBSITE

USERNAME

PASSWORD

NOTES

WEBSITE

USERNAME

PASSWORD

NOTES

WEBSITE

USERNAME

PASSWORD

NOTES

WEBSITE

USERNAME

PASSWORD

NOTES

P

WEBSITE

USERNAME

PASSWORD

NOTES

WEBSITE

USERNAME

PASSWORD

NOTES

WEBSITE

USERNAME

PASSWORD

NOTES

P

WEBSITE

USERNAME

PASSWORD

NOTES

WEBSITE

USERNAME

PASSWORD

NOTES

WEBSITE

USERNAME

PASSWORD

NOTES

Q

WEBSITE

USERNAME

PASSWORD

NOTES

WEBSITE

USERNAME

PASSWORD

NOTES

WEBSITE

USERNAME

PASSWORD

NOTES

WEBSITE

USERNAME

PASSWORD

NOTES

WEBSITE

USERNAME

PASSWORD

NOTES

WEBSITE

USERNAME

PASSWORD

NOTES

Q

WEBSITE

USERNAME

PASSWORD

NOTES

WEBSITE

USERNAME

PASSWORD

NOTES

WEBSITE

USERNAME

PASSWORD

NOTES

WEBSITE

USERNAME

PASSWORD

NOTES

WEBSITE

USERNAME

PASSWORD

NOTES

WEBSITE

USERNAME

PASSWORD

NOTES

R

WEBSITE

USERNAME

PASSWORD

NOTES

WEBSITE

USERNAME

PASSWORD

NOTES

WEBSITE

USERNAME

PASSWORD

NOTES

WEBSITE

USERNAME

PASSWORD

NOTES

WEBSITE

USERNAME

PASSWORD

NOTES

WEBSITE

USERNAME

PASSWORD

NOTES

R

WEBSITE

USERNAME

PASSWORD

NOTES

WEBSITE

USERNAME

PASSWORD

NOTES

WEBSITE

USERNAME

PASSWORD

NOTES

WEBSITE

USERNAME

PASSWORD

NOTES

WEBSITE

USERNAME

PASSWORD

NOTES

WEBSITE

USERNAME

PASSWORD

NOTES

S

WEBSITE

USERNAME

PASSWORD

NOTES

WEBSITE

USERNAME

PASSWORD

NOTES

WEBSITE

USERNAME

PASSWORD

NOTES

S

WEBSITE

USERNAME

PASSWORD

NOTES

WEBSITE

USERNAME

PASSWORD

NOTES

WEBSITE

USERNAME

PASSWORD

NOTES

S

WEBSITE

USERNAME

PASSWORD

NOTES

WEBSITE

USERNAME

PASSWORD

NOTES

WEBSITE

USERNAME

PASSWORD

NOTES

WEBSITE

USERNAME

PASSWORD

NOTES

WEBSITE

USERNAME

PASSWORD

NOTES

WEBSITE

USERNAME

PASSWORD

NOTES

T

WEBSITE

USERNAME

PASSWORD

NOTES

WEBSITE

USERNAME

PASSWORD

NOTES

WEBSITE

USERNAME

PASSWORD

NOTES

WEBSITE

USERNAME

PASSWORD

NOTES

WEBSITE

USERNAME

PASSWORD

NOTES

WEBSITE

USERNAME

PASSWORD

NOTES

T

WEBSITE

USERNAME

PASSWORD

NOTES

WEBSITE

USERNAME

PASSWORD

NOTES

WEBSITE

USERNAME

PASSWORD

NOTES

T

WEBSITE

USERNAME

PASSWORD

NOTES

WEBSITE

USERNAME

PASSWORD

NOTES

WEBSITE

USERNAME

PASSWORD

NOTES

U

WEBSITE

USERNAME

PASSWORD

NOTES

WEBSITE

USERNAME

PASSWORD

NOTES

WEBSITE

USERNAME

PASSWORD

NOTES

WEBSITE

USERNAME

PASSWORD

NOTES

WEBSITE

USERNAME

PASSWORD

NOTES

WEBSITE

USERNAME

PASSWORD

NOTES

WEBSITE

USERNAME

PASSWORD

NOTES

WEBSITE

USERNAME

PASSWORD

NOTES

WEBSITE

USERNAME

PASSWORD

NOTES

U

WEBSITE

USERNAME

PASSWORD

NOTES

WEBSITE

USERNAME

PASSWORD

NOTES

WEBSITE

USERNAME

PASSWORD

NOTES

V

WEBSITE

USERNAME

PASSWORD

NOTES

WEBSITE

USERNAME

PASSWORD

NOTES

WEBSITE

USERNAME

PASSWORD

NOTES

WEBSITE

USERNAME

PASSWORD

NOTES

WEBSITE

USERNAME

PASSWORD

NOTES

WEBSITE

USERNAME

PASSWORD

NOTES

V

WEBSITE

USERNAME

PASSWORD

NOTES

WEBSITE

USERNAME

PASSWORD

NOTES

WEBSITE

USERNAME

PASSWORD

NOTES

WEBSITE

USERNAME

PASSWORD

NOTES

WEBSITE

USERNAME

PASSWORD

NOTES

WEBSITE

USERNAME

PASSWORD

NOTES

WEBSITE

USERNAME

PASSWORD

NOTES

WEBSITE

USERNAME

PASSWORD

NOTES

WEBSITE

USERNAME

PASSWORD

NOTES

WEBSITE

USERNAME

PASSWORD

NOTES

WEBSITE

USERNAME

PASSWORD

NOTES

WEBSITE

USERNAME

PASSWORD

NOTES

WEBSITE

USERNAME

PASSWORD

NOTES

WEBSITE

USERNAME

PASSWORD

NOTES

WEBSITE

USERNAME

PASSWORD

NOTES

WEBSITE

USERNAME

PASSWORD

NOTES

WEBSITE

USERNAME

PASSWORD

NOTES

WEBSITE

USERNAME

PASSWORD

NOTES

WEBSITE

USERNAME

PASSWORD

NOTES

WEBSITE

USERNAME

PASSWORD

NOTES

WEBSITE

USERNAME

PASSWORD

NOTES

X

WEBSITE

USERNAME

PASSWORD

NOTES

WEBSITE

USERNAME

PASSWORD

NOTES

WEBSITE

USERNAME

PASSWORD

NOTES

X

WEBSITE

USERNAME

PASSWORD

NOTES

WEBSITE

USERNAME

PASSWORD

NOTES

WEBSITE

USERNAME

PASSWORD

NOTES

X

WEBSITE

USERNAME

PASSWORD

NOTES

WEBSITE

USERNAME

PASSWORD

NOTES

WEBSITE

USERNAME

PASSWORD

NOTES

Y

WEBSITE

USERNAME

PASSWORD

NOTES

WEBSITE

USERNAME

PASSWORD

NOTES

WEBSITE

USERNAME

PASSWORD

NOTES

WEBSITE

USERNAME

PASSWORD

NOTES

WEBSITE

USERNAME

PASSWORD

NOTES

WEBSITE

USERNAME

PASSWORD

NOTES

Y

WEBSITE

USERNAME

PASSWORD

NOTES

WEBSITE

USERNAME

PASSWORD

NOTES

WEBSITE

USERNAME

PASSWORD

NOTES

WEBSITE

USERNAME

PASSWORD

NOTES

WEBSITE

USERNAME

PASSWORD

NOTES

WEBSITE

USERNAME

PASSWORD

NOTES

Z

WEBSITE

USERNAME

PASSWORD

NOTES

WEBSITE

USERNAME

PASSWORD

NOTES

WEBSITE

USERNAME

PASSWORD

NOTES

Z

WEBSITE

USERNAME

PASSWORD

NOTES

WEBSITE

USERNAME

PASSWORD

NOTES

WEBSITE

USERNAME

PASSWORD

NOTES

Z

WEBSITE

USERNAME

PASSWORD

NOTES

WEBSITE

USERNAME

PASSWORD

NOTES

WEBSITE

USERNAME

PASSWORD

NOTES

Z

WEBSITE

USERNAME

PASSWORD

NOTES

WEBSITE

USERNAME

PASSWORD

NOTES

WEBSITE

USERNAME

PASSWORD

NOTES